C&M VOL.1
USAF, ANG, & NASA MARKINGS

COLORS & MARKINGS OF THE F-106 Delta Dart

Bert Kinzey

C&M VOL.1

Aero Publishers, Inc. U.S.A.

Arms and Armour Press London - Melbourne

This book is produced by Bert Kinzey, who has sole responsibility for the contents and layout except that all contributors are responsible for the security clearance and release of all materials submitted. Published and printed in the United States by Aero Publishers, Inc., and in London and Melbourne by Arms and Armour Press.

CONTRIBUTORS:

Marty Isham
Ray Leader
Don Spering
Wally Van Winkle
The U.S. Air Force
Doug Barbier
Warren Munkasy
George Cockle
Don Linn
Convair
Mike Campbell

Most photographs in this book are credited to their contributors. Photos with no credit indicated were taken by the author.

Printing 9 8 7 6 5 4 3 2 1

Published in United States by

Aero Publishers, Inc.
329 W. Aviation Road
Fallbrook, CA 92028

Library of Congress Cataloging in Publication Data

Kinzey, Bert.
Colors & Markings of the F-106 Delta Dart
(C & M ; Vol. 1)
1. Delta Dart (Jet Fighter Plane) I. Title.
II. Title: Colors and Markings of the F-106 Delta Dart. III. Series.
UG1242.F5K523 358.4'3 1984 84-2952
ISBN 0-8168-4525-5

Published in Great Britain by

Arms and Armour Press
Lionel Leventhal Limited
2-6 Hampstead High Street
London NW3 1QQ
and in Australasia at
4-12 Tattersalls Lane
Melbourne, Victoria 3000
and in South Africa at
Sanso Centre
8 Adderley Street
P.O. Box 94
Cape Town 8000

British Library Cataloging in Publication Data:

Kinzey, Bert
F-106 Delta Dart—(C & M ; v.1)
1. Delta Dart (Jet Fighter Plane)
2. Fighter planes—Models
I. Title II. Series
623.74'64 UG1242.F5
ISBN 0-85368-645-9

Printed and Published in the USA by Aero Publishers

The painting on the front cover depicts F-106A, 59-0127, as it appeared in 1972 while with the 48th FIS. The aircraft was flown by Captain Malcolm Emerson (now a major). The painting was done by John W. Clark specifically for the cover of this publication.

For information concerning the availability of prints of the cover painting by John W. Clark, please write to:

Aerospace Art
3445 North Cramer Street
Milwaukee, Wisconsin 53211

INTRODUCTION

A 318th FIS F-106A, 59-0110, from McChord AFB, Washington, is shown as it appeared in 1981. The unit converted to F-15s in 1983. (Mayo via Barbier)

Since this is the first volume of the Colors & Markings Series, it seems appropriate to include here an introduction to the series as well as the F-106 Delta Dart which this book covers. On the inside front cover is an explanation of our purpose in this series, which is to provide a reasonably priced, continuing series covering the paint schemes and markings that adorned important aircraft in aviation history.

Each book in this series will be a little different in format as dictated by the aircraft being covered. In this book, the F-106 is presented unit by unit. Every unit to fly the Delta Dart is included in the chronological order in which those units received the aircraft. Units that were redesignations of earlier units are covered immediately after the squadron that was redesignated. All ADWC aircraft are covered together. Active Air Force units are covered first, followed by the Air National Guard units that have flown the "Six". NASA aircraft are also included. The sixteen-page color section is separate from the rest of the book, and covers most of the units with color coverage. Some of the photographs, both color and black and white, are rare and are as much as twenty-three years old. While some of the older photographs show their age, they are included because of their historical significance. While we could have filled these pages with recent and beautiful photographs, it seemed more important to include the older photographs which show markings that were carried by the F-106 in its early years, but have long since been replaced with newer ones.

As we stated on the inside front cover, it is impossible to make a sixty-four page book the definative work on the markings carried by the Delta Dart, but every unit to fly the aircraft is included. In order to provide coverage of an aircraft which has been in service for a quarter of a century, a lot of research had to be done, and assistance had to be received from many people. Most notable of these include Marty Isham, who many consider to be the leading expert on ADC and its aircraft, and Doug Barbier, whose contribution was also significant. The efforts and

The first F-106A is seen in overall ADC gray, FS 16473. Although a Southeast Asia camouflage scheme was designed for the F-106, there is no evidence that it was ever applied to an aircraft. With few exceptions, such as NASA aircraft and the "City of Jacksonville" bicentennial aircraft, all F-106s were painted ADC gray.(Convair)

photographs from Ray Leader, Warren Munkasy, Don Spering, Wally Van Winkle, and George Cockle should also be noted. Without the help of these people, the coverage presented would be far less extensive than it is.

Although produced in fewer numbers than any of the other "Century Series," the F-106 had more than its share of admirers. It is considered by many to be one of the most beautiful of all fighter designs. On the pages that follow is the most complete coverage ever presented on the markings carried by the Delta Dart, the aircraft that has served as a front line interceptor for a quarter-century. As with all of the books in this series, the captions tell the story. A special effort has been made to include the dates each unit received the F-106, and the date it either deactivated or transitioned to a newer aircraft. As of press time all active units but two have either been deactivated or have made the transition, and the Delta Dart's days are numbered. It will soon pass into aviation history having never fired a shot in anger, but having defended America's skies proudly for many years.

Included in this publication are almost two hundred photographs of the F-106 of which sixty-five are in color. Very few have ever been published before, and together they provide extensive coverage of the markings carried by "The Ultimate Interceptor."

F-106A, 56-0455, the fifth F-106 built, is shown in the markings of Air Force Systems Command. The band and cat on the tail are florescent red. The photo was taken on September 9, 1966. (Isham collection)

F-106B, 57-2512, is shown in the markings of the 4786th Test Squadron. The insignia on the tail is a disc with "Mach III Plus" written through a YF-12A silhouette which is firing two missiles. Colors for these markings are unknown. (Leader collection)

539th FIS

The 539th FIS was the first unit to receive an F-106. It began conversion from the F-86L in July 1959, and flew the F-106 until deactivated on June 1, 1967. During this time the squadron was based at McGuire AFB, New Jersey.
(USAF via Barbier)

Right side view of a 539th FIS aircraft in flight. Note the buzz number on the fuselage as carried by the F-106 early in its operational life. This is a very early photo as evidenced by the lack of an IR sensor fairing on the nose. This particular aircraft crashed on April 22, 1969, while serving with the 460th FIS.
(Isham collection)

Another early 539th FIS aircraft is seen in this photograph, which bears evidence that the marking on the vertical tail was the same on both sides. (Compare with photo at left.) When compared to the photo above, it can be seen that an addition has been made to the tail markings. *(Isham collection)*

This photo, taken in 1967, shows the later markings carried by the 539th FIS. The markings include a gold star with a blue outline, and a blue lightning bolt with a gold outline. For color photos of both the early and late 539th markings, see page 30.
(Isham collection)

498th FIS

Although the 539th FIS was the first unit to receive the F-106, it was the 498th FIS at Geiger Field, Washington, that was the first unit to become operational and stand alert in the aircraft. The unit was known as the Geiger Tigers, and converted from the F-102 during the second half of 1959. In May 1963, the squadron moved to McChord, and then to Paine Field in June 1967. Finally, on September 30, 1968, they moved to Hamilton AFB and were redesignated the 84th FIS. This photo shows the early markings carried by the 498th, and it features a "Geiger Tiger" in a disc of yellow, white, and blue. The rudders are red, and 57-2482 has a dark blue fin cap. A similar color photo appears on page 30. *(NORAD via Isham)*

The disc with the "Geiger Tiger" can be seen on this aircraft in a photo taken in September 1967. By this time the markings had changed considerably from those shown in the photo above. Tail colors are red, white, and blue with white stars. *(Isham collection)*

84th FIS

The 84th FIS was activated on September 30, 1968, and was a redesignation of the 498th FIS, as that unit moved to Hamilton AFB. On September 1, 1973, the 84th FIS moved to Castle AFB. In mid 1981 it was redesignated the 84th FITS, and was equipped with T-33s. The 84th FIS was named the "Black Panthers," and a black panther replaced the tiger in the disc on the tail. Otherwise the markings remained the same as they had with the 498th FIS. This photo was taken in the summer of 1974. (Isham collection)

During the 1976 bicentennial celebration, the speed brake was painted blue with a white disc surrounded with white stars. A red "76" was painted in the disc. ((USAF via Barbier)

This close-up of the tail of 59-0063 shows the black panther in the disc, replacing the earlier "Geiger Tiger." A color photograph of an 84th FIS aircraft appears on page 30. (Leader collection)

84th FIS, "Black Panthers" refuel from a KC-135 tanker. Note that the flash from the disc has been changed from that shown in the photo above. On the speed brake, the white disc, surrounded with white stars, now has a red "84th" in it. Note also how the serial number is down into the red on the tail markings. This is the latest variation of the markings carried by the 84th before TAC badges replaced the black panther insignia on the tail. (USAF via Isham)

27th FIS

The 27th FIS converted from the F-102 to the F-106 on October 1, 1959, and moved to Loring AFB, Maine, from Griffiss AFB. It was redesignated the 83rd FIS (covered on the next page) on July 1, 1971. Here, two 27th FIS aircraft fly close formation. 59-0032 has the cartoon character Alfred E. Neuman painted on the nose. *(Isham collection)*

F-106B, 59-0149, is shown in 27th FIS markings. The ADC badge is in the triangle on the tail on the right side. *(Leader collection)*

The tail markings for the 27th FIS consisted of a band of yellow (FS 13538) and black (FS 17038) checkerboard squares. A yellow arrowhead design, outlined in black and having three black stars, was imposed over the checkerboard. The squadron insignia consisted of a falcon in a white and yellow disc surrounded with a broad red circle. A yellow scroll beneath the disc read, "27th Fighter Interceptor Squadron," and "Falcons" was written in the disc between the falcon's wings. The pitot probe had yellow and black bands. *(Isham collection)*

83rd FIS

The 27th FIS was deactivated and redesignated the 83rd FIS at Loring AFB on July 1, 1971. However it was deactivated only a year later on June 30, 1972. (Geer via Isham)

An 83rd FIS F-106 takes off from Loring AFB in the spring of 1972. (Isham collection)

Markings for the 83rd FIS included dark blue and white bands on the tail. A gold chevron is painted over the bands and is outlined in black. Three black spades are in the corners of the chevron. The squadron insignia consists of an ultramarine blue disc with a gold horseshoe and a red lightning bolt passing through a black and white ace of spades. (Taylor via Isham)

95th FIS

One of the best known F-106 squadrons was the 95th FIS, known as "Mr. Bones and Company." It converted to the Delta Dart in the fall of 1959 while at Andrews AFB, Maryland. It moved to Dover AFB, Delaware, on July 1, 1963, and was deactivated on January 31, 1973. (Isham collection)

The original markings for the 95th FIS can be seen in these two photos. The squadron insignia consisted of a blue disc with a white skull and hand, a yellow lightning bolt, and a black hat and cane. Buzz numbers were carried. (Left, Isham collection, right, via Barbier)

The 95th FIS was one of the F-106 units sent to stand alert in Korea during the Pueblo crisis. Here, two aircraft are shown at Osan AB in 1970. Note the different shades of blue in the tail markings of the two aircraft. Specifications called for the blue to be FS 15102, and the yellow to be FS 13538. (via Barbier)

The last markings carried by the 95th included the same disc insignia as before, but it was smaller in size and placed in a yellow lightning bolt outlined in black. The ADC badge was on the opposite side. This photo was taken at William Tell 1972. Color coverage of the 95th FIS markings is on page 31. (Isham collection)

456th FIS

The 456th FIS began conversion from the F-102 to the F-106 during the first half of 1960 while located at Castle AFB, California. On July 18, 1968, it moved to Oxnard, and was redesignated the 437th FIS. This is the ops officer's aircraft as seen in September 1962. It crashed on August 27, 1963, while with the 498th FIS. The crash was a mid-air collision with a B-57. The tail is yellow (FS 13538) outlined in black with black stripes on the rudder. Yellow stripes outlined in black are on the fuselage, and the triangular name plate is also yellow outlined in black. The three stripes at the base of the tail are red, white, and blue from top to bottom.

(Knowles via Isham)

This later photograph of a 456th FIS aircraft shows some changes from the markings on the aircraft in the photo above. There are more stripes on the rudder, and the buzz number has been deleted. There is no flash coming from the squadron insignia. The tail bands and rudder stripes are now a blue (FS 15044) instead of black.

(Isham collection)

437th FIS

The 456th FIS was redesignated the 437th FIS on July 18, 1968, as the unit moved from Castle AFB to Oxnard AFB. But the unit had the distinction of being an F-106 unit for the shortest period of time. Less than ten weeks later, on September 30, 1968, the unit was again redesignated the 460th FIS. Colors of the 456th FIS were carried through the 437th FIS period, and became the first markings for the 460th FIS as seen below. So far as can be determined, no distinctive 437th markings were ever carried. "Colors & Markings" would like to hear from any reader who knows of any. These two aircraft are pictured in the time frame that these unit redesignations took place. (Isham collection)

460th FIS

This aircraft, an ex 456th FIS and 437th FIS F-106, is shown in the old 456th markings but with the "Cave Tigrim" Tiger insignia of the 460th FIS. These markings were the first used by the 460th FIS. (Isham collection)

The 460th FIS changed its markings to those seen on this page. Basic colors were yellow (FS 13538) and black, and the striped rudder was retained from earlier markings carried by the 456th and 437th FIS.

(Isham collection)

F-106A, 58-0779, is shown as it appeared in 1972 at Grand Forks AFB, North Dakota.

(Taylor via Barbier)

The tiger insignia consisted of a black, yellow, white, & red tiger on a blue shield. There was a gold scroll with black letters for the words "Cave Tigrim." The ADC badge was on the right side of the tail.

460th FIS F-106s often carried a yellow rectangle outlined in black under the standard armament rectangle. The markings on the fuel tank are noteworthy, and were standard on 460th FIS aircraft with these markings. A color photograph of a 460th FIS aircraft appears on page 31.

319th FIS

The 319th FIS converted from the F-89J Scorpion to the F-106 in January 1960 at Bunker Hill AFB, Indiana. They moved to Homestead AFB, Florida, in February 1963, and converted to the F-104A. Then, on July 1, 1971, the 71st FIS was redesignated as the 319th FIS, and the 71st squadron designator was given to TAC. Since the unit was equipped with the F-106, the 319th FIS has the distinction of being the only unit to fly the Delta Dart twice. *(Isham collection)*

Members of the 319th FIS pose with their squadron insignia. Note that the ADC badge is on the right side of the tail as evidenced by the aircraft in the background. This photo was taken in April 1972, during the unit's second time around with the F-106. *(Isham collection)*

This close-up of the tail shows the 319th FIS markings to good effect. The tail flash is blue (FS 15102) outlined in black. However, a gold outline was also used. The disc is yellow outlined in black. The black and white cat holds a red and white bomb. Under the disc is a white scroll outlined in red with red letters reading, "We get ours at night." *(Isham collection)*

5th FIS

The 5th FIS moved to Minot AFB, North Dakota, and began conversion to the F-106 on February 1, 1960. As of the release date of this book, they are still there some twenty-four years later, still in the F-106. The squadron is known as the "Spitten Kittens." *(Geer via Isham)*

Left: This close-up of the tail shows the earlier markings carried by the 5th FIS to good effect. The fin flash is yellow (FS 13538) outlined in black. The squadron insignia consists of a face of a Lynx in yellow/orange, black, and white, a blue disc, yellow lightning flashes, and white stars. *(Leader collection)*

Below: This in-flight shot shows that the ADC badge was located on the right side of the tail. *(USAF via Barbier)*

Later tail markings carried by 5th FIS Delta Darts are seen in this photo. However the usual fuel tank markings are missing. Markings are yellow (FS 13538) outlined by dark blue lightning flashes. The stars are also dark blue. This photo was taken in November 1978. (Barbier)

Right: An F-106A of the 5th FIS seen in the later markings. (Leader collection)

Below: This photo shows the markings carried by the 5th FIS at the time of release for this book. The TAC badge is on both sides of the tail, and the squadron insignia is on the nose just aft of the radome. Color photos of 5th FIS aircraft are on page 32. (Leader)

318th FIS

The 318th FIS converted from the F-102 to the "Six" in April 1960. Known as the "Green Dragons," they are based at McChord AFB, Washington. They flew the F-106 until 1983 when they began transition to the F-15. In this photo, the 325th Fighter Wing's badge is on the tail, while the 318th FIS insignia is on the nose. The tail design is light blue (FS 15102) and dark blue (FS 15044). *(Isham collection)*

Left: This 1963 photo shows an F-106B of the 318th FIS landing. The squadron insignia has been moved to the tail design, replacing the 325th Fighter Wing design. *(Isham collection)*

This photo, taken in April 1971, shows a later tail marking with the ADC badge on a white disc. The squadron insignia was on the opposite side. *(Mayo via Barbier)*

Shown here is a variation on the design in the photo at left. While the basic marking remains the same, it is now outlined in white to make it stand out more. Also note the markings on the fuel tank. *(Leader collection)*

A third tail design is shown in this photo. The dark blue and light blue colors remained the same throughout. (Barbier)

Shown here is the left side with the last tail design carried by 318th FIS F-106s. Later, the TAC badge replaced the squadron insignia and ADC badge within the design, and the squadron insignia was moved to the nose. Color photos of 318th FIS aircraft are on page 32. (via Barbier)

94th FIS

The 94th FIS transitioned from the F-86L to the F-106 during the first half of 1960. At that time the unit was based at Selfridge AFB, Michigan. It served a tour in Korea, then was transferred to Wurtsmith AFB upon its return to the United States on December 1, 1969. The famous "Hat in the Ring" squadron was redesignated the 2nd FIS on July 1, 1971. This photo shows the original 94th FIS markings. The bands on the tail are red and white with a blue V. The hat is red, white, and blue. The shooting star on the nose is a light blue with the pilot's name in black. *(Isham collection)*

This F-106B, also from the 94th FIS, has the ADC badge on the left side of the tail. This is most unusual. This photo was taken in 1962. *(Geer via Isham)*

In 1966, this 94th FIS F-106A had the First Fighter Wing badge on its tail. The "Hat in the Ring" insignia is located on the nose. (Isham collection)

Here two 94th FIS aircraft in-flight refuel as they return from their Korean deployment. The "Hat in the Ring" insignia is on a white disc on a yellow (FS 13538) tail band. The band is outlined in black. Color photos of 94th FIS aircraft are on page 33. (USAF via Isham)

2nd FIS

The 2nd FIS came into being on July 1, 1971, as a redesignation of the 94th FIS. The last 94th FIS markings were retained in the form of a yellow band outlined in black. The "Hat in the Ring" insignia was replaced with that of the 2nd FIS, which was known as the "Horney Horses." The unit remained based at Wurtsmith AFB, Michigan, until deactivated on March 31, 1973. (Barbier)

Left: This close-up of the tail shows the 2nd FIS "Horney Horse" insignia that replaced the "Hat in the Ring" insignia when the 94th FIS was redesignated. (Geer via Isham)

The right side markings remained the same as they had been with the 94th FIS. The ADC badge was located in a white disc within the yellow tail band. Markings of the 2nd FIS are shown in color on page 33. (Barbier)

438th FIS

The 438th FIS converted from the F-102 to the F-106 during the first half of 1960. At that time the unit was based at Kincheloe AFB, Michigan. It was redesignated the 49th FIS and moved to Griffiss AFB on September 30, 1969. The squadron insignia is a Walt Disney Productions duck on a yellow disc. (USAF via Isham)

This photo shows another 438th FIS aircraft as it appeared in the fall of 1967. A black and white design has been added to the tail. (See close-up below.) (Buchanan via Isham)

An earlier scheme used by the 438th was like the earlier scheme used by the 94th FIS and the 71st FIS. It consisted of red and white stripes, a blue V, and the 438th insignia within the V. (Geer via Isham)

This close-up of the tail markings on the aircraft above shows that the duck is facing aft on this aircraft. In the top photo it is facing forward. (Buchanan via Isham)

49th FIS

The 438th FIS was redesignated the 49th FIS at Griffiss AFB, New York, on September 30, 1969. It is still operational in the F-106 as of press time for this book. The 49th FIS is known as the "Green Eagles." This photograph was taken shortly after the 49th FIS was activated, and the green and white feathers can be seen on the tail. The rest of the well known eagle design has not yet been added. *(Morris via Isham)*

The entire "Green Eagle" is shown in this photograph. For colors, see the photographs on page 34. The flash on the fuel tank is yellow outlined in black, and matches the lightning bolt that the eagle is holding.
(Mayer via Barbier)

THE DELTA DART IN COLOR

F-106A, 56-0453, was the third F-106 built. Like other early "Sixes" that were used for testing, it carried high visibility orange on the nose, wings, and tail and "Convair F-106A" on the nose. The aircraft is seen here as it appeared at Edwards AFB, California, in May 1958. Later it was assigned to ADWC, and in 1979 to the 48th FIS. (Balzer)

Another aircraft with high visibility markings on the tail and wings is F-106B, 57-2513, as seen here in February 1977. The markings on the fuel tank reads, "San Antonio A.L.C. (Leader)

FEATURE SQUADRON - THE 48th FIS

At William Tell 1978, the 48th FIS had several aircraft with nose art. F-106A, 56-0458, was "Thunderchicken," and a close-up of the nose art is shown below. *(Leader)*

Close-up of "Thunderchicken" on the nose of 56-0458. *(Leader)*

F-106A, 59-0123, was named "Patience." *(Leader)*

Close-up of "Patience" on 59-0123. *(Leader)*

F-106A, 59-0145, had "TAZ" painted on the nose. "TAZ" has appeared on several 48th FIS aircraft.(Leader)

Close-up of "TAZ" as displayed on 59-0145. (Leader)

"Broadway Byrd" as seen on 59-0133. (Leader)

"Broadway Byrd" was 59-0133. "USMC" was painted under the design as shown above. (Leader)

FEATURE SQUADRON - THE 87th FIS

At the 1972 William Tell weapons meet, the "Red Bulls" of the 87th FIS displayed some interesting nose art. 57-0230 was "Big Red 1," and had a bull on the nose. *(Munkasy)*

F-106A, 59-0094, was "Bones Crusher." Perhaps the 84th FIS was making a reference to beating the 95th FIS "Mr. Bones and Company" at the competition. *(Munkasy)*

"Lurch IV" was 59-0089. Again, a red bull is shown on the nose, but this time in an interesting pose. *(Munkasy)*

Close-up of "Lurch IV" showing the detail of the red bull character. *(Munkasy)*

F-106A, 59-0091, was "The City of Marquette." Also note the markings on the fuel tank. *(Munkasy)*

Close-up of the nose art on 59-0091. The map is of the northern part of Michigan. *(Munkasy)*

On November 6, 1976, 59-0053 was photographed in these markings. This aircraft has the name, "The City of Marquette" on the nose gear door, but is not the same aircraft so named on the previous page. Note the different fuel tank markings as compared to those used at William Tell 1972. *(Leader)*

With one fuselage band, 59-0051 is named "Big Red." It carried a snorting red bull on the nose and a bicentennial "pretzel" next to it. The name was on the nose gear door. *(Leader)*

This January 1981 photo shows F-106A, 59-0095, on the transit ramp at Ft. Campbell. The head of a bull is on the nose, and pilot and crew names are on the nose gear door. Bear intercept markings are located below the armament rectangle, and are shown in the photo to the right. By this time, ADC units had been turned over to TAC, and the TAC badge is on the tail. *(Campbell)*

Close-up of the nose markings on 59-0051. The pilot's and crew names appear between the horns of the bull. "Big Red" appears on the nose. *(Leader)*

Close-up of Soviet Tu-95 Bear intercept markings on the aircraft shown in the photo to the left. Unlike the Soviet Union, the United States does not shoot down military aircraft in peacetime, much less airliners. However, a large number of such intercepts are made on a continual basis as the Soviet Union probes U.S. defenses. *(Cambell)*

ACTIVE AIR FORCE SQUADRONS

Colors carried by the 539th FIS as of mid 1959 are seen in this photo. *(Isham collection)*

This photo, taken on May 20, 1967, at McGuire AFB, shows the last markings used by the 539th FIS. *(Isham collection)*

Colors of the 498th FIS, "Geiger Tigers" are seen in this photo. *(Isham collection)*

Colors of the 84th FIS are seen in this photo of F-106A, 59-0056. The photo was taken on August 12, 1978. *(Logan via Leader)*

This May 1965 photo shows markings carried by the 95th FIS, "Mr. Bones and Company," as of that date. *(Isham collection)*

Later markings used on 95th FIS aircraft as shown in this June 29, 1970, photograph at Andrews AFB. Note the different blues in the tail colors of the aircraft. *(Isham collection)*

At William Tell 1972, the 95th FIS displayed its last markings. The "Mr. Bones" insignia is in a yellow lightning bolt. *(Munkasy)*

The black and yellow markings of the 460th FIS can be seen in this September 1972 photo. The "Cave Tiger" insignia is in the white disc on the tail. *(Brewer via Barbier)*

Markings of the 5th FIS, as of January 16, 1971, are seen in this photo of F-106A, 57-0237. This aircraft crashed on May 8, 1974. (Isham collection)

The later 5th FIS markings are shown in this January 1978 photo. The squadron insignia is within the yellow area on the tail. (Barbier)

On October 19, 1980, with ADC units transferred to TAC, the 5th FIS markings showed some changes. The TAC badge is on the tail, and the squadron insignia is on the nose. Markings have been added to the fuel tanks. (Rogers via Isham)

The 318th FIS displayed these markings at William Tell 1972. Note the markings on the fuel tank. The squadron insignia is within the tail markings. (Munkasy)

This October 24, 1982 photo shows several changes to 318th FIS markings. The tail markings have been changed, and the TAC badge is included. The "Green Dragon" squadron insignia is on the nose. The marking on the fuel tanks has also been changed. (Leader)

The famous "Hat in the Ring" markings of the 94th FIS are on the white disc within the yellow band. This photo was taken in October 1970. (Buchanan via Isham)

94th FIS F-106As are shown returning to the United States from deployment to Osan AB, Korea. (USAF via Barbier)

F-106A, 57-2465, is shown at Wurtsmith AFB, Michigan, in the markings of the 94th FIS. (via Barbier)

The only change that the 2nd FIS made to 94th FIS markings, when the latter unit was redesignated, was to replace the "Hat in the Ring" marking with the "Horney Horse" in the white disc on the left side of the tail. This photo was taken in September 1972. (Leader)

329th FIS markings are shown in this June 1965 photo taken at George AFB. (Isham collection)

Markings of the 71st FIS, "Flying Fists," are shown in this December 1969 photo. Note the "Flying Fist" insignia within the tail flash. (Isham collection)

Markings of the 49th FIS "Green Eagles" are shown on F-106A, 59-0021. This aircraft was the commander's aircraft of the 21st NORAD Region, and it carries command stripes on the fuselage and special fuel tank markings. The name "El Jefe" is on the nose. BG Price died in a crash in this aircraft on May 15, 1973, just over two months after this photo was taken. (Isham collection)

The latest markings to be carried by the 49th FIS are shown in this photo. The TAC badge is on the tail, and yellow lightning flashes are on the fuel tanks. The "Green Eagle" marking remains on the tail.(Leader)

AIR DEFENSE WEAPONS CENTER

ADWC markings as used in 1974 are shown in this photo. Cameras are located on the wing pylons. *(Isham collection)*

In 1976, F-106B, 59-0165, was the personal aircraft of General "Chappie" James, CINC NORAD. Note the changes in the markings as compared to the photograph above. This aircraft was destroyed by a fire at Tyndall AFB on February 27, 1980. *(Isham collection)*

Close-up of the nose markings on General "Chappie" James aircraft. *(Leader)*

An F-106A in ADWC markings as seen in October 1978. Note the change in the fuel tank markings as compared to those on F-106B, 59-0165, above. *(Leader)*

AIR NATIONAL GUARD UNITS

The beautiful markings of the California ANG consisted of a white tail with a gold bear and red band with "California" within. This photo was taken at William Tell 1978. (Leader)

At William Tell 1982, the colorful California ANG markings were gone, and were replaced with these rather plain markings.

The present markings of the Massachusetts ANG are shown in this photo. (Isham collection)

Michigan ANG F-106s are seen here in colorful yellow and black markings. The aircraft in the foreground, F-106A, 580772, is "Defiance," and has nose art that shows a mouse with a lot of spunk! (Barbier)

Montana ANG markings have remained basically the same since the unit first received the Delta Dart. This photo was taken at William Tell 1982.

F-106A, 57-2485, from the Montana ANG is shown at William Tell 1978 with three fuselage stripes. (Leader)

Florida ANG markings have remained the same since the squadron received the F-106. (Barbier)

Earlier New Jersey ANG markings are shown in this photo taken on June 12, 1976. (Isham)

Present New Jersey ANG markings are shown in this photo. Three small bear intercept markings are below the windscreen. (Van Winkle)

BICENTENNIAL DARTS

The most colorful "Six" ever was the "City of Jacksonville," F-106A, 58-0760, which was painted in these colors for the American bicentennial celebration by the Florida ANG. *(Leader)*

The 318th FIS painted F-106A, 58-0776, in these bicentennial markings. The aircraft was called "The Freedom Bird." *(Leader collection)*

The "Spirit of 76" was the bicentennial aircraft for the 49th FIS. The "Green Eagle" remains on the tail. This photo was taken in March 1976. *(Swanberg via Leader)*

Taken on April 17, 1976, this photo shows that the "Spirit of 76" had been removed from the aircraft. Other markings remain the same. *(Woodoo via Isham)*

NASA

An unusual sight is this bare metal F-106B belonging to NASA. This is N816NA as seen in blue and gray below. This photo was taken on February 9, 1983. *(Van Winkle)*

This photo, taken on April 30, 1982, shows N816NA in NASA colors. The markings were the same on both sides of the aircraft. *(Leader)*

These two photos show F-106B, N607NA (57-2507), in two different blue and white color schemes. The photo on the left was taken on September 28, 1982, and the one on the right was taken in 1978 while the aircraft was at Selfridge ANGB, Michigan. *(Left, Wolf via Van Winkle, right via Barbier)*

F-106A, 57-0235, was the twenty-fourth Delta Dart built, and served with NASA from September 4, 1958, to December 14, 1959. It later served with the 87th FIS. Note the early boundary layer fences on the wings which were later replaced with a single slot. *(Isham collection)*

NASA F-106A, N607NA, serial 57-2507, is shown in flight. A color photograph of this aircraft appears on the previous page. *(NASA via Barbier)*

F-106B, 57-2516, became NASA NF-106B, N616NA. It was used for numerous tests. Here it is shown with three engines while at Selfridge ANGB during the time the Michigan ANG flew the F-106. Colors are the same as those shown on the previous page. *(Balogh via Barbier)*

329th FIS

The 329th FIS converted from the F-102 to the F-106 during the second half of 1960 while at George AFB, California. It was deactivated on May 1, 1967. This is an early photo as indicated by the lack of an IR sensor, the old style wheels, and the buzz number on the fuselage. A color photograph of a 329th FIS aircraft is shown on page 34.
(Isham collection)

This photo shows the markings on the right side of a 329th FIS F-106A. The ADC badge replaces the squadron insignia on the tail, but otherwise the markings remain the same. This is a later photo than the one at the top of this page as evidenced by the IR sensor fairing on the nose and the newer style main gear wheels. By this time the buzz numbers were no longer carried. *(Leader collection)*

An F-106B from the 329th is shown in this photo. Each squadron had F-106Bs assigned with their F-106As. They were used for proficiency training, umpiring air-to-air combat training, and they retained the full combat capability of the F-106A.
(Leader collection)

71st FIS

The 71st FIS converted from the F-102 during the second half of 1960 at Selfridge AFB, Michigan. It moved to Richards-Gebaur AFB, Missouri, on January 15, 1967, then to Malmstrom AFB, Montana, on July 8, 1968. When the 71st squadron designator was assigned to TAC on July 1, 1971, the unit was redesignated the 319th FIS. (See page 15.) The 71st FIS was known as the "Flying Fists." In this 1962 photo, taken at Selfridge AFB, the familiar red and white bands and blue V are seen on the tail. The First Fighter Wing crest is in the V, and the squadron insignia is on the nose. Today the Michigan ANG, flying F-4Cs, still sits alert in these same barns. (Isham collection)

The 71st FIS carried these markings for the 1965 William Tell competition. Note the arrow and apple marking on the tail and the squadron insignia on the nose. (Candid Aero-File photo via Isham collection)

These markings were carried by the 71st FIS in May 1966 at Selfridge AFB. The First Fighter Wing badge is on the tail, and the squadron insignia is on the nose. (Isham collection)

By 1967, the squadron insignia had been moved to the tail, replacing the First Fighter Wing badge. (Isham collection)

This 1968 photo shows the blue flash outlined in black on the tail. The squadron insignia is on the left side. (Isham collection)

Later markings carried by the 71st FIS consisted of a blue (FS 15102) flash outlined in black. This photo, taken in 1968, shows the ADC badge on the right side of the tail. A color photo showing these markings is on page 34. (Leader collection)

11th FIS

The 11th FIS converted from the F-102 to the F-106 in October 1960. It was redesignated the 87th FIS on September 30, 1968. Both the 11th and 87th FIS were known as the "Red Bulls." Again, the red and white stripes with blue V are present. The squadron insignia has a red and white bull charging from a white cloud and blue sky. The border is red with white letters reading, "11th Fighter Interceptor Sqdn." *(Isham collection)*

This 1961 photo shows the early markings carried by the 11th FIS. The pilot's and crew chief's names are on the tail. This aircraft crashed on November 26, 1972, while serving with the 87th FIS. *(Isham collection)*

Two 11th FIS F-106As are seen at William Tell 1963. The closer aircraft has a shamrock nose art, color unknown. *(Isham collection)*

During the 1966-67 time frame, the 11 FIS changed to these markings. A red (FS 11136) tail flash, outlined in black, replaced the red and white stripes with the blue V. The squadron insignia remained on the tail.
(Isham collection)

F-106A, 59-0096, from the 11th FIS taxis past the alert barns at Duluth IAP, Minnesota, in 1967.
(USAF via Barbier)

87th FIS

The 87th FIS came into being when the 11th FIS was redesignated on September 30, 1968, at Duluth. They moved to K.I. Sawyer AFB on May 1, 1971, and are still operational there as of press time for this book. They are one of the best known F-106 units, and are covered in the color section on pages 28 and 29. As seen in this photo, the first markings used by the 87th FIS were the same as those used by the 11th FIS except that the squadron insignia was changed. *(Isham collection)*

Right: The red tail flash is outlined in black as it was with the 11th FIS. Note that the red flash comes down further on the tail on this aircraft than it does on the other two aircraft pictured on this page. *(Leader collection)*

Right side view of an 87th FIS aircraft as photographed at K.I. Sawyer AFB, Michigan, in August 1972. The ADC badge is on the right side of the tail. *(Barbier)*

The well known bull's head marking on the tail is present in this William Tell 1972 photograph. Readers should note slight differences in the size and shape of this distinctive marking, as well as differences in the eyes and angle of the horns. (Isham collection)

This 1978 photo shows the red and white markings on the fuel tanks and a bull's head on the nose. Red and white stripes are on the fuselage, and a bicentennial "pretzel" marking remains on the nose. (Barbier)

This aircraft was named "The City of Marquette," and had green and white nose art and red and white fuel tank markings at William Tell 1972. (Leader collection)

This F-106B has a bull marking of a noticably different style than others on this page. (Barbier)

In April 1978, 59-0095 carried the red bull on the tail, the bull's head on the nose, and the red and white fuel tank markings. *(Barbier)*

These F-106s from the 87th FIS fly in formation during the summer of 1976. The lead aircraft has three stripes on the fuselage, the left wing aircraft has two stripes, and the right wing aircraft has one. The number four aircraft has none. Two aircraft have the ADC badge, and two do not. *(Isham collection)*

This close-up shows the red bull marking with the TAC badge. *(Cockle)*

This F-106B has the markings carried by the 87th FIS after ADC's squadrons came under TAC. The TAC badge is on both sides of the tail. *(Cockle)*

48th FIS

The 48th FIS converted from the F-102 to the F-106 during the second half of 1960. It flew the Delta Dart from Langley AFB until it became the first F-106 unit to transition to the F-15 in the spring of 1982. A detachment from the 48th FIS was stationed at Homestead AFB for some time. This early photo shows 59-0135 with the 48th FIS insignia on the tail.
(Isham collection)

This photo shows a worn ADC badge on the right side of the tail. These markings were often stickers stuck on the aircraft.
(Spering)

A broad white band, outlined in black, and black rudder stripes became the standard 48th FIS markings by the late 60's.
(Isham collection)

The last markings carried by the 48th FIS Darts were white and blue. Markings for the fuel tanks were added. Until ADC units were turned over to TAC, the squadron insignia was on the left side of the tail, and the ADC badge remained on the right. *(Spering)*

The ADC badge has been removed after the deactivation of that command. The "Taslanglian Devil" cartoon character is on the tail markings. See pages 26 and 27 for colors. *(Spering)*

After ADC units came under TAC, the TAC badge was placed on both sides of the tail. The squadron insignia was moved to the nose. *(Cockle)*

AIR DEFENSE WEAPONS CENTER

The Air Defense Weapons Center has flown the F-106 since the aircraft became operational with the first squadrons. This aircraft carries the markings of the 73rd Air Division. *(USAF via Barbier)*

This aircraft also carries the markings of the 73rd Air Division. These markings consist of a black band, gold lightning bolt, and a red and white chevron. The photo was taken on May 18, 1963. *(Isham collection)*

The 4756 ADW badge is on this ADWC aircraft as photographed in 1964. *(Isham collection)*

General Agan, the commander of ADC, flew 57-2541 as his personal aircraft. The chevron is red, white, and blue, and the stripes on the tail are red and white. The fuel tank markings are also red, white, and blue. These markings are representative of those used by ADWC in 1969. (Isham collection)

Newer markings are shown in this March 1976 photo. The chevron is gone from the tail, and a blue field with white stars has been added ahead of the rudder stripes. The rudder stripes are more narrow, and take up less of the rudder than those in the photo above. The fuel tank markings remain the same. (Isham collection)

Now that ADWC is under TAC, the TAC badge has been placed on the white disc on the tail. The ADWC insignia is on the nose, and the red, white, and blue markings on the fuel tanks have been changed from the style in the photos above. This photo was taken on April 12, 1980. ADWC aircraft are shown in color on page 35.(Spering)

CALIFORNIA ANG

The California ANG, 194th FIS, received the F-106 in the summer of 1974. It still flies the Delta Dart from Fresno as of press time for this book. *(Barbier)*

This F-106B, 57-2523, saw service with the 71st, 94th, and 2nd FIS, as well as the Michigan ANG, before being assigned to the California ANG. The California ANG Darts had a white tail with a golden bear. At the base of the tail was a red band with the word "California" in black. A color photograph of these markings is on page 36. *(Barbier)*

This line-up of California ANG aircraft was seen at the 1980 William Tell weapons meet. *(Leader)*

This June 1981 photo shows the same markings, but the usual red stripe on the fuel tank is missing. *(Van Winkle)*

Many aviation photographers covering Wiliam Tell 1982 were disappointed to see the colorful white and red tail with the golden bear replaced with a plain blue band outlined in black. The word "California" is in the black letters in the band. A TAC badge is on the left side of the tail, and the unit insignia is on the right. A blue stripe, also outlined in black, is on the fuel tanks with black letters reading "194th FIS." With colorful markings disappearing from so many aircraft, it is a real shame to see California's beautiful earlier markings discarded. (Cockle)

This close-up photo shows the blue band and unit insignia on the tail. Also note the "194th FIS" on the fuel tank marking. (Cockle)

This photo, taken at William Tell 1982, shows the left side of a California ANG F-106. Note the TAC badge on the tail.

MASSACHUSETTS ANG

The Massachusetts ANG, 101st FIS, received ex-95th FIS Darts in 1972. The unit still flies the "Six." This photo was taken at Otis ANGB, Massachusetts, in 1973. *(via Barbier)*

The first markings carried by the Massachusetts ANG consisted of a green band, outlined in white and green, with white letters spelling out "Massachusetts" on the tail. *(via Barbier)*

Newer markings carried by Massachusetts aircraft are light blue and white. The unit marking, carried on the left side of the tail, is a white gull on a blue disc. The blue disc is outlined with white, black, and yellow rings, from the inside out. This photo was taken on May 4, 1978. (Leader)

The newer style ANG badge can be seen on the right side of the tail in this photo. Also note the "Cape Cod" marking on the fuel tank. (Leader)

This F-106B was photographed at William Tell 1978 in Massachusetts ANG markings. Two small Firebee drone kills are painted in red on the nose. See page 36 for color photograph of Massachusetts ANG markings. (Leader)

This close-up shows the name plate on a Massachusetts ANG aircraft. The same blue and white colors are used. Behind the names is a cartoon representing a bear and a duck. (Leader)

MICHIGAN ANG

The Michigan ANG, 171st FIS, received ex-2nd FIS F-106s when that unit deactivated in April, 1973. It flew the Delta Dart until 1978 when it converted to F-4Cs. The squadron became known as "Six Pack," as evidenced by the marking on the fuel tank. *(Barbier)*

The colors for the Michigan ANG are yellow and black, and are among the most popular applied to any ANG aircraft. Here, 58-0793 is about to land at the unit's home field, Selfridge ANGB, Michigan. *(Barbier)*

F-106A, 58-0772, is shown approaching the runway at Selfridge ANGB in May 1978. *(Barbier)*

This photo shows 59-0109 in Michigan ANG colors. The fuel tank is missing the usual "Six Pack" marking. *(Barbier)*

The Michigan ANG is the 171st FIS, of the 191st FIG. However no unit badges were carried on the aircraft. *(Leader)*

Here, F-106B, 59-0150, is shown as it appeared in June 1977. Michigan ANG markings remained unchanged during the entire time the unit flew the "Six." See page 37 for a color photo of Michigan ANG aircraft. *(Geer via Leader)*

MONTANA ANG

The Montana ANG, 186th FIS, 120th FIG, received the F-106 during the first week of May 1972. Most of the aircraft came from the 460th FIS. The unit still operates the F-106. This photo shows three F-106As of the Montana ANG in flight over Glacier National Park shortly after the unit transitioned to the F-106. Note that the aircraft still have the old style canopy with the overhead bracing. ***(Mont. ANG via Barbier)***

In the photograph at the top of this page, aircraft number 17 is an F-106A. In this photo, number 17 is F-106B, 57-2517, and this photograph was taken some ten years later. Note that the 17 is on both the nose and tail of the aircraft. The fuel tank markings are clearly visible in this photo. ***(Cockle)***

The Montana ANG markings have remained the same since the unit received the F-106. The new style ANG badge has replaced the older style (compare this photo to the one at the top of the page), and minor differences exist. For example, the aircraft number for this aircraft appears only on the aft fuselage and not on the nose as is the case with number 17 above. Color photographs of Montana ANG markings can be found on page 37. ***(via Barbier)***

FLORIDA ANG

The Florida ANG received the F-106 in 1974, replacing the F-102. Although scheduled to transition out of the "Six" in 1983, plans were changed, and the unit will fly the Delta Dart for a while longer. The Florida ANG unit flying the F-106 is the 194th FIS, 125th FIG, and it is based at Jacksonville. This photograph was taken at William Tell 1976. *(Spering)*

Markings for the Florida ANG are simple, consisting of a blue tail band outlined in white. A white lightning bolt is in the blue band, and the word "Florida" is in blue script above the band. Fuel tank markings are sometimes present as seen in the top photo. Although their regular markings are quite plain, it was the Florida ANG that painted the spectacular "City of Jacksonville" as seen on page 39. A Florida ANG aircraft is seen in color on page 38. *(FANG via Barbier)*

NEW JERSEY ANG

The New Jersey ANG, 119th FIS, 177th FIG, based at Atlantic City, New Jersey, received the F-106 during the first week of February 1973. They still fly the "Six" over ten years later. Most aircraft are ex-95th FIS aircraft. This photo, taken in May 1976, shows the earlier markings carried by the New Jersey ANG aircraft. Markings are in red, and the unit insignia is on the left side of the tail. *(Spering)*

Here, a New Jersey ANG F-106 is shown about to land. It has the earlier markings, and the newer ANG badge is on the right side of the tail. This photo was taken in the spring of 1978. *(Barbier)*

Newer markings carried by the New Jersey ANG are seen in this photo. Again, the markings are red, and the fin flash is bordered in white on the leading and bottom edges. "Jersey Devils" has been replaced by "New Jersey" on the tail. *(Isham collection)*

These two photographs, both taken in 1981, show the new markings for New Jersey. However, note that both aircraft in the photo at left have the unit insignia on the tail, while the aircraft in the photo at right does not. Other photos show some aircraft with the insignia and others without it at the same point in time. See page 38 for color photographs of both New Jersey ANG schemes. *(Both photos, Linn)*

THE FIRST AND THE LAST

The photo above is of the first F-106 produced, 56-0451. It was usually seen in overall ADC gray, and is now on display at the Air Force Museum at Wright-Patterson AFB, Ohio. Below is 59-0148, which was the last F-106A built. It served with the 318th FIS, 325th FG, and crashed on April 22, 1969.

(Top, Convair, Bottom, Isham collection)